J 636.3
Paladino,
Catherine.

Spring fleece

$14.45

DATE			

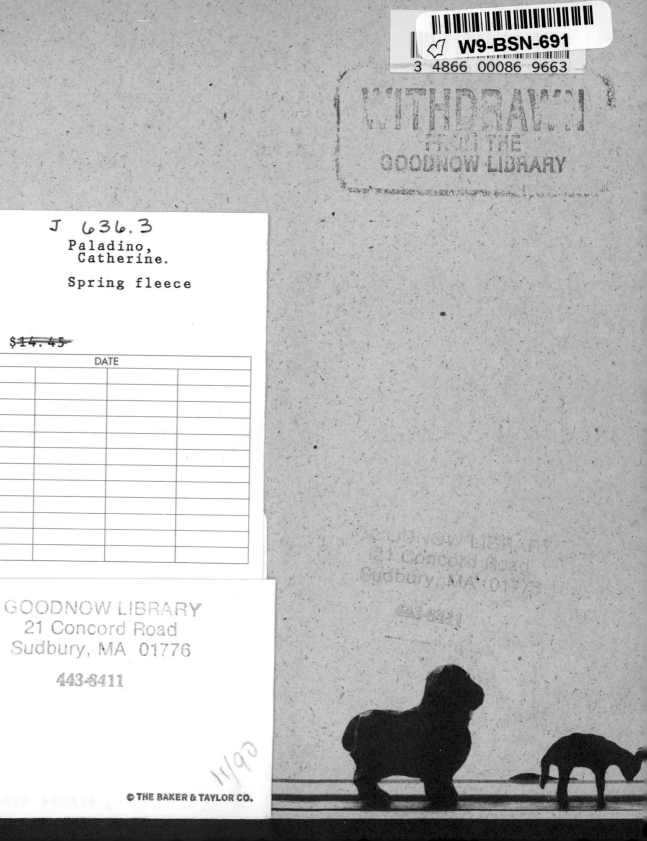

Spring Fleece
A Day of Sheepshearing

by Catherine Paladino

Little, Brown and Company

BOSTON • TORONTO • LONDON

Special thanks to:
Carol and Kevin, for the goodness of their work;
Carole and David Presberg of Woolgather Farm,
in Merrimac, Massachusetts, and Nancy and Ralph Hughes of
Four Winds Farm, in Oakham, Massachusetts,
for their kindness; and to the sheep,
for their everlasting patience.

First Edition

Library of Congress Cataloging-in-Publication Data

Paladino, Catherine.
Spring fleece : a day of sheepshearing / Catherine Paladino.
p.   cm.
Summary: Text and photographs follow two sheep shearers through
their day of rounding up sheep, shearing them, and bundling the
fleeces, and establish connections between the fleeces and the wool
making up many articles of clothing.
ISBN 0-316-68890-8 (lib. bdg.)
1. Sheep-shearing—Juvenile literature.   2. Wool—Juvenile
literature.   [1. Sheep-shearing.   2. Wool.]   I. Title.
SF379.P35   1990
636.3'145—dc20   89-12820
                                           CIP
                                           AC

10 9 8 7 6 5 4 3 2 1
BP

Joy Street Books are published by
Little, Brown and Company (Inc.)

Published simultaneously in Canada
by Little, Brown & Company (Canada) Limited

Printed in the United States of America

For Mom and Dad, with love.

◆✕◆

*I*t's a chilly day, not quite spring. The March wind blows, and stubborn patches of snow still stick to the ground. Early this morning the sheep at Woolgather Farm run excitedly toward their barn. Today their long coats will be shorn. The shepherd's dog chases them into a pen where they'll wait till the shearing begins.

The sheepshearers will visit both this farm and another New England farm today. They will clip the wool coats the sheep have worn all year.

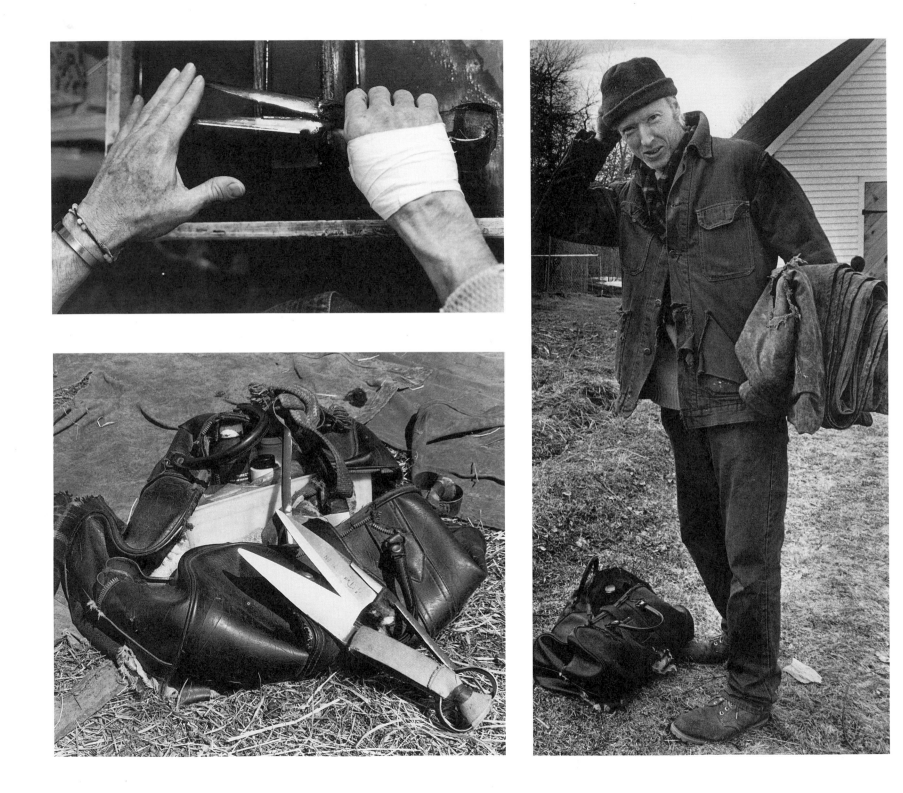

In their cottage far away the shearers prepare for shearing day. Kevin gathers their tools — three pairs of long shears called blades. One pair is for him, another for his wife, Carol, and the third pair is extra, in case the others get dull. They are the same kind of simple blades that sheepshearers used hundreds of years ago. Kevin sharpens them on a flat stone and tucks them into his soft leather sack.

"C'mon, Cane!" Carol calls to their dog. "We're going shearing!" She climbs into the truck and Cane leaps onto her lap. Kevin loads the gear in the back of the truck. He looks at his map. It's a long way to their first stop, at Four Winds Farm. Time to get going.

❖❖❖

At Four Winds Farm, four big rams wait to be sheared. Rams are male sheep. They're bigger than ewes, which are female sheep, and grow to weigh more than two hundred pounds. An angry ram can be difficult or even dangerous to handle, so shepherds usually keep fewer rams than ewes on their farms. Mostly, rams are kept for breeding with ewes. In a small flock of fewer than twenty sheep, there might be only one ram.

The Romney rams at Four Winds Farm have very thick wool coats. They probably will be happy to have them shorn off for the spring and summer. But this is not the main reason to shear sheep. Wool is really a crop, grown for a specific purpose. Just as some farmers grow grain for people to eat, shepherds grow wool for people to make into clothing, carpets, and works of art. The wool harvest begins in late winter or early spring. In New England, shearing season can start as early as February and run as late as July.

Before sheep farming, when all sheep were wild creatures, they did not have the heavy wool coats they have today. Wild sheep looked more like goats. Their only wool was a thin layer underneath an outer layer of coarse, straighter hairs. Ever since we discovered the value of wool thousands of years ago, we have been breeding sheep to purposely make their woolly layer heavier and more lustrous. Sheep breeders try to produce lambs with high-quality wool by choosing parent sheep with the best fleeces. The best fleeces have good sheen and an even texture.

The shearer's job is to harvest the wool for the shepherd. Some shearers use electric clippers, which shave very close to the sheep's skin. Hand shearing, the method Carol and Kevin use, leaves about a half-inch layer of wool on the sheep's body. This keeps the sheep warm and means that hand shearing can begin before the last snow melts — just as long as the shorn sheep are kept out of cold rains. But shearing with electric clippers cannot be done until warmer weather arrives.

Carol and Kevin will shear the four Romney rams out in the pasture. They spread canvas tarps on the ground to keep the wool from getting dirty when it falls from the sheep. The first ram to be shorn is named George Washington. His coat, called a fleece, is weathered and rough-looking on the outside, but underneath it's clean and soft and white.

Carol leads George Washington over to the tarp. He's very strong, but Carol knows how to handle him firmly. Kevin takes one of the other rams onto another tarp. Expert sheepshearers like Carol and Kevin follow the same set of steps with each sheep they shear. But not every sheep behaves the same way. Some are more nervous than others. Rams are usually stubborn and obstinate, while ewes act more skittish. The shearers know this. They treat the sheep kindly, taking care not to upset them. A good shearer does his job without hurting the sheep.

First, Carol must turn George Washington onto his backside. Sheep are easier to handle with their feet off the ground, because then they don't struggle or try to run. Eventually some sheep even appear to relax while they're being shorn, like someone getting a haircut from a trusted barber.

"That's a good sheep," Carol says to George Washington. She cups one hand under his chin and grabs his tail end with the other. Then she leans the heavy sheep against her knee, turning him over with a quick but gentle motion. As he topples onto his rear, his thick wool acts like a cushion. With all four feet in the air, George Washington looks like a big, floppy, raggedy doll.

Next Carol clips his hooves with trimmers. Sheep hooves grow the way our toenails do but only need trimming about every six months. Now George Washington is ready for shearing.

Carol begins by clipping the wool between George Washington's front legs, an area called the brisket. Next comes the belly wool, which she clips and lays aside. The rest of his fleece will come off in one piece. Meanwhile, Kevin shears another ram in the same way.

Then Carol clips carefully down his legs and up over his short tail, which is called the dock. Sheep naturally have long tails, but some shepherds have them cut short, or docked, when the sheep are young lambs. Long tails tend to collect dirt and manure, so shepherds feel docking helps keep the sheep cleaner.

The next blow, or stroke of the shearer's blades, is the neck blow. Carol clips from the brisket up to George Washington's right cheek. Then she shears the wool on top of his head, called the topknot.

When the delicate areas around his face are done, Carol can shear more quickly. "*Zzzzitcha zzzzitcha zzzzitcha!*" go the blades, open and shut in her strong, sure grip. Now down the shoulder, where the wool is best, and across George Washington's left side. Now up his back in the long swift strokes called long blows. The shepherd watches as Carol's blades plow through the fleece as though it were a pile of snow. But Carol is always careful not to nick the sheep's skin. If she does, when she's finished shearing she will dab antiseptic on the cut to help it heal.

The only wool that remains to be shorn is on George Washington's right side. This is called the whipping side, because the shearer sweeps the blades over it quickly, back and forth. "*Zzzzit-cha zzzzitcha zzzzitcha zzzzitch.*" Finally the fleece is free. George Washington scrambles to his feet, leaving his creamy white fleece behind him in a mound.

Nearby, Kevin works on the second ram. As he clips, one of the unshorn rams watches curiously. It takes about an hour to finish shearing all four of the rams. When the shearing is done, the four fleeces get put into four big boxes. They will be sold later this spring at a county fair. Carol and Kevin shake out the tarps and gather their tools. It's time to break for lunch.

Inside the farmhouse the shepherd has a good meal of soup and breads and cheeses ready for the shearers. Afterward Carol and Kevin say good-bye and travel on to their next stop: Woolgather Farm.

The sky has turned cloudy and the air cold, so the shearing at Woolgather Farm must be done indoors. Friends and neighbors have come to help with the special chores of shearing day. When Carol and Kevin arrive, the flock of sixteen ewes waits for them in its pen, where it was herded earlier. A friend of the shepherd coaxes the ewes into a corner of the pen, called the crowding pen. Sheep are easier to catch in a crowding pen than in a big open pasture.

"Hi, sheep-sheep!" Carol says to the ewes, while she and Kevin spread the tarps on the floor of the empty shearing pen. Then they each take one ewe to opposite ends of the pen. With arms outstretched, they grasp the sheep and gently turn them over. Working together, Carol and Kevin shear two sheep at a time.

Visitors perch on a wall of the shearing pen to watch. Carol begins shearing one of the white sheep. It's important to keep any dark wool that falls on the tarps away from the white wool. Black or brown wool in a white fleece is considered a contaminant. For this reason, in a flock of many colors the white sheep usually get shorn first. Carol starts with Angelica; Kevin with her niece, Rosa.

This year there are only a few white ewes in the flock. Most of the sheep are various shades of brown. The sun bleaches their wool cocoa brown on the outside, but underneath it might be as dark as semi-sweet chocolate. As the sheep get older, this rich brown color turns smoky gray.

Knitters and weavers buy fleeces from Woolgather Farm because they like to work with yarns made from sheep of different colors. They can use the natural wool colors to weave or knit patterns without having to dye their yarn.

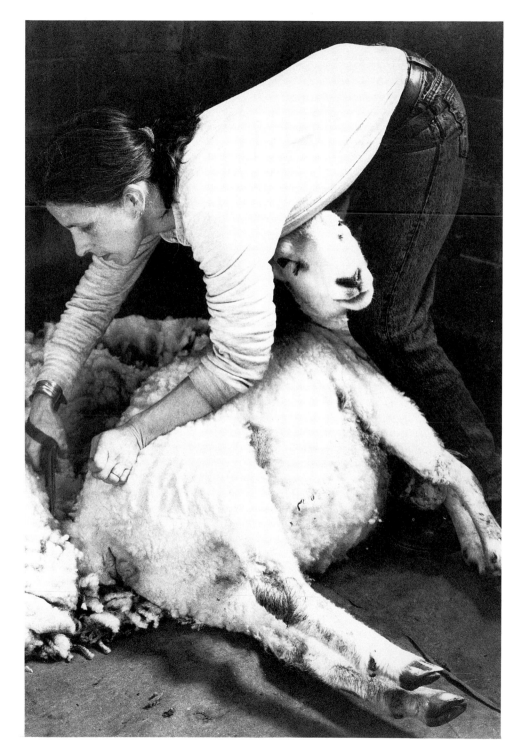

Wool piles up around the shearers' feet. Carol and Kevin work fast. Every ten minutes another fleece slips from a sheep like an unbuttoned coat.

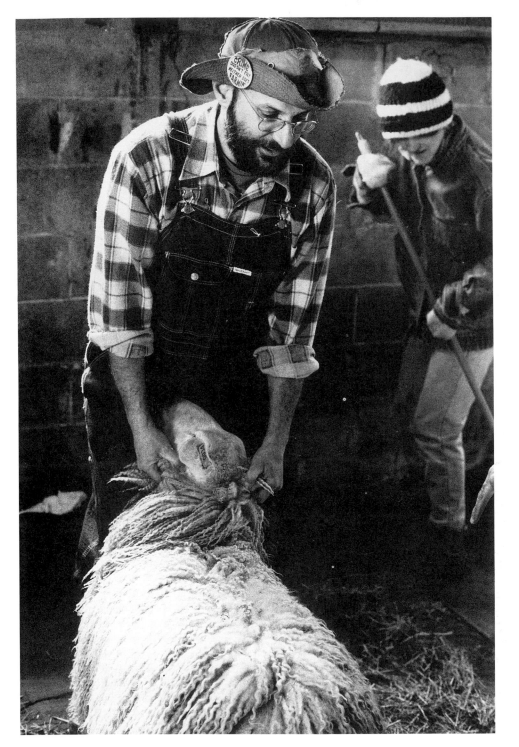

"Wool away!" Carol calls after each fleece is shorn. "Bring me another sheep." A friend who came to help leads another ewe into the shearing pen while two other neighbors carry away the fleece from the last sheep.

■✕■

Upstairs, the newly shorn fleeces are spread out one at a time on the clean-swept floor. Many hands help with both the "skirting" — removing dirty clumps of wool from the edges of the fleece — and the "picking," plucking out loose pieces of hay, twigs, and dried manure. Short or matted bits of wool may not be good for spinning, but they can be washed and used for stuffing pillows.

Freshly shorn wool still feels warm from the heat of the sheep's body. It makes your fingers shiny if you rub it, the way butter would. That's because it contains a greasy substance called wool wax. Glands in the sheep's skin produce wool wax. It keeps their skin soft and their wool supple. Wool wax can keep our skin soft, too. We make lanolin from it to put in soaps and creams.

After skirting and picking, the fleece gets bundled up and tied with twine or put in a burlap sack. Then the shepherd weighs and labels each one with a name tag — Rosa, Angelica, Belle, Sweetbriar, Cleo. Though no two fleeces are exactly the same, each one weighs between eight and ten pounds. But this is not actually the weight of the wool alone. Dirt and oils account for up to half the fleece's weight. When the dirt and oils are washed out of the wool, the weight of the fleece goes down. A ten-pound fleece, for instance, might weigh only five pounds after washing. Usually, a fleece is washed before it's spun into yarn. If a fleece has lots of oil in it, the unwashed wool is sticky and difficult to spin. But sometimes a spinner spins wool directly from an unwashed fleece. This is called spinning in the grease.

 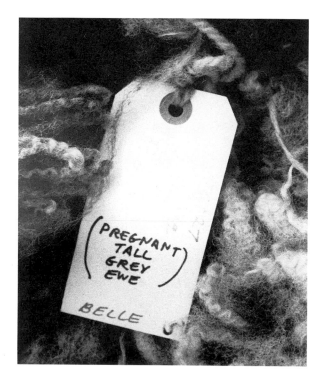

Wool grows on sheep in clumps called locks. The locks are held together by wispy strands that look like cotton candy. Tiny scales on each wool fiber, like scales on a fish, make the fibers cling together by catching hold of each other. This is why we are able to spin wool into long, unbroken strands of yarn.

The scales on wool fibers also enable us to make a special kind of woolen fabric that's neither spun nor woven: felt. Felt is made by rubbing wool fibers together with soap and water on a hard surface. The scales interlock and hold the fabric together. We can make slippers, hats, and even jackets from felt.

When you pat a sheep, it's not like patting a straight-haired dog or cat, whose hair lies flat. The hairs on a sheep grow like coiled springs. This makes the wool push back on your palm when you pat it. This waviness of wool is called its crimp. Some fleeces have a very tight crimp, while others have almost no crimp at all.

Like hair, wool fibers can be fine or coarse. To make a sweater, a knitter would choose a fine wool with a tight crimp. But to make a rug, a weaver would use a coarse wool with a loose crimp. Coarse wool would itch if you wore it next to your skin, while fine wool feels soft. A rug made of coarse wool is more durable than one made of fine wool. Also, tightly crimped wool is stretchy and good for knitting, while loosely crimped wool lies flatter and is good for weaving.

Crimp makes wool elastic, which keeps woolen garments from wrinkling. If you stretch crimpy wool, it springs back into shape when you let go. A wool suit that's gotten wrinkled will smooth itself out when you hang it up overnight. The wool fibers return to the shape they had before they got wrinkled.

Crimp also makes wool a good insulator against cold or heat. The zigzag of wool fibers creates tiny air pockets between them. The trapped air protects you from the outside temperature, so wool fabric can keep you warm in winter and cool in summer.

After the wool is washed and before it gets spun into yarn, it has to be "carded" to remove the tangles. Carding is like combing your hair; it's done with wire brushes. Carded wool can then be spun on a spinning wheel or on a simple spindle. The spinner's fingers guide the fibers from a tuft of carded wool toward the growing strand of yarn. When one handful is spun, the spinner adds another to the end of the yarn by twisting the fibers together.

After the yarn is spun a weaver threads a loom with yarns running lengthwise and weaves over and under them with yarns running crosswise. A complex floor loom is used for weaving wide blankets and rugs, as well as fabric. Narrower scarves and belts can be woven on a simple loom called a backstrap loom, which loops around the weaver's waist.

A ten-pound fleece from one sheep yields enough spun wool after washing to knit a couple of sweaters, or a dozen pairs of mittens, or two dozen hats. Or, instead, the yarn could be woven into one small blanket.

We like to use knitted or woven wool for our clothes and blankets because it repels water naturally. Since each wool fiber is covered with a waxy surface that sheds water, water droplets run off it. But wool fibers also have tiny holes in them that will gradually soak up water vapor or moisture. In summer, wool clothing absorbs sweat, keeping us cool and dry. A wool coat in winter absorbs the cold dampness from the air, making us warm and dry. Even if your wool socks or mittens get wet, they will keep you fairly dry, because wool absorbs the moisture and keeps it away from your skin.

It's nearly four o'clock when Carol and Kevin finally finish shearing at Woolgather Farm. Now it's time to fill the manger with hay and the trough with grain. The sheep are especially hungry, since they weren't fed any breakfast this morning. Because sheep become nervous and excited on shearing day, a full belly might make

them feel sick. So the shepherd waits to feed them until after they're shorn.

With their long coats gone, the sheep take up less space and can squeeze close together at their manger. All of their mouths crunching grain at once sounds like rain falling on a barn roof.

◆◆◆

Carol and Kevin get ready to leave. While Carol gathers the tools, Kevin takes Cane for a short walk before their long trip home. Spring is coming, and there will be lots more wool to harvest around New England. Carol and Kevin will keep on shearing right through the summer.

It's almost lambing time for some of the ewes at Woolgather Farm. After shearing, their pregnant bellies look especially round without their fleeces covering them. Soon they will give birth to their lambs. As they chew their oats and hay, just a few hours after shearing, they have already begun the business of growing back their fleeces for next spring.